Spiritual Exercise

Spiritual Exercise

Lance Carden

RESOURCE *Publications* · Eugene, Oregon

SPIRITUAL EXERCISE

Resource Publications
An Imprint of Wipf and Stock Publishers
199 W. 8th Ave., Suite 3
Eugene, OR 97401

www.wipfandstock.com

PAPERBACK ISBN: 978-1-5326-9129-4
HARDCOVER ISBN: 978-1-5326-9130-0
EBOOK ISBN: 978-1-5326-9131-7

Manufactured in the U.S.A.   08/08/19

To Lexa and Laura

Contents

Preface

These poems need no introduction. Nor do they require of readers an academic or religious connection of any kind—just a yearning for spiritual growth.

Vision

My First Love

On the back of a building
    a block away,
I could barely make out the words
    HOTEL VENUS
the residue of some previous identity,
    still legible
    vertically
    in dark blue or black
through recent coats of paint
    in brighter hues.

Each time I noticed this,
    my eyes would squint
    in search of other
    visible bits,
& recently, during such an event,
    I suddenly asked my wife,
if she knew the word "palimpsest,"
    whose spelling
    & meaning
    I could no longer attest.

"A palimpsest," she recalled,
    "is when something
    is covered over or buried,
but still partially perceptible."

For me, palimpsest had been consigned
    to some deep alcove
    of the mind,
where high-school Spanish lies
    in deep decay
    under heavy
Germanic, Greek, & French layers
    of subsequent,
    supposedly "higher"
education.

Now, as I am laboriously re-learning
    a little *español*,
I marvel over another vanished treasure,
    obtained & lost
    quite early:
an ability to speak with God
    as naturally & simply
    as with a kitten
    or a bullfrog.

Visionaries

For the great artists
   of all time,
   it's not
   so much
that they impart
   so well
   the worlds
   we see,

but that they see
   in part
   some worlds
   we *don't*,

& thus rehearse
   for all
   of us
the glories of the universe.

Through the Heart

Philosophers & scholars
    have their place,
but reason won't save
    the human race.

Till we start thinking,
    or being led,
through open hearts
    not the head,
we won't reflect
    from above
that long-lost prospect
    of heaven & love.

Apocalypse

Time seems fated
     to entirely
eliminate
     all that is evil
     or equivocal
     in our little world
& then by design
     to evaporate
     at the speed
of all-absorbing light.

No calendar can
     possibly
     measure
the sure-footed march
     of good
as it evolves
     from so-called
     human law
     & justice
into love & brotherhood.

Tall Tale

This organic life—
    a tall-tale told—
unfolds but slowly
    only to be
disposed & forgot,
    a carcass
    of thought
used & abandoned,
    dust-to-dust,
by all that's ever
    truly us.

Biblical Confession

That our sacred Bible is
    a marvelous mess
    of inconsistency
    & historicity,
I freely do confess.

But I must also stress:
    This cobbled tome
    probably represents
    in prose & verse
our best prospect
    to ever know
    our hidden selves,
    & grasp the grandeur
of the universe.

Our Bios

Like the real histories
of the world,
temporarily
hidden
from human view,
most of
our true
biographies
have yet
to be written.

When the so-called
dots of life
are fully & finally
connected,
they'll fit together
in steadily
curving lines,
& all lives will align
in concentric
circles.

In the Whirl

They say that a ballerina
    can maintain
    her balance
while spinning round & round
    hurrah, hurrah!
  by fixing her gaze
on some object in space
    again, again
    turn after turn,
& a Turkish whirling dervish
    does much the same
    hurrah, hurrah!
by staring piously inward,
    as into
    a mirror,
& locking eyes with Allah.

No Kiddin'

All those "li'l chil'uns"

    go'na seem

    so wise

when we so-called "adults"

    start to

    see 'em

    soul-ly

through Spirit eyes.

Lighthouse

I caught its beacon
    from the sea,
certain it was
    sent for me.
I knew not then
    what it meant
just a port, some hope
    of safety,
but I set my course
    toward that beam,
which seemed so vital,
    pure, & clean.

That brilliant shaft
    I knew not then
is radiant Spirit,
    guiding men.

Been in this light
    of Truth & Love
now two-score years
    & more,
but still my eyes
    well up in tears
the way it quells
    my sordid fears.

In the Garden

As a bright slanting sun
   darts in & out
of elegantly white
   cumulous clouds
   over & over,

this whole lovely Eden
   flattens, softens
   loses life,
then comes bouncing back
   again & again,

like some giant marionette
   responding
   to the string,
& illustrating a fine point
   Philo made:

". . . that trained minds
   like shining suns
should keep our senses
   in the shade." *

Oh, for the mental wiring
   & for that holy day
when the inspirations
   hold fast
& then *never* fade away.

Allegorical Interpretation 2.30

Poet's Work

The highest work
    of the poet—
not exclusively,
    or even
    mainly
    on paper—
is to translate what we
    blindly see
as merely matter
    back into
the Spirit sphere.

Deity

One God

God's oneness is his allness;
   no two, three, or four.
God's allness is his oneness,
   no after, no before.

Could anything be plainer?
   He has made it known.
There can be no other;
   she is God alone.

Genesis One

I read again & again
 these invaluable verses
preceding the mist, the dust,
 the inevitable curses.

I sing again praises of Elohim,
 the mighty Creator
both of & in this lyrical hymn.

This Lord is without & within
 those perfect forms
she shapes & spins:

No force nor creature
 can resist his call;
she's Lord of all,
 & still *more* than all.

Wonder Words

Forced to shove
    what's known
    of God
into a single word,
    "Love," I find.

If the line
    be drawn
    at two,
I submit:
    "One Mind."

If we extend that
    to three:
then "*Sine Qua Non.*"

The One Mind

Shine on me & all mankind
all the riches of one Mind;
help us feel that joy profound
& hear the angel voices' sound.

Bring us news which goes beyond
what on Earth is cheered or crowned;
teach us peace & law unbound
from human thought, which shops around.

Let us yield ourselves to God,
understand what Jesus taught,
find the wholeness we have lost,
harmony that can't be bought.

True ideas here are sought
& other thoughts best forgot.
God is *one* Mind, right & kind;
at one in God, ourselves we find.

My Friend

He's my friend
        every day;
a friend in need is God
        in deed.

She makes quick work
        of all my tasks;
keeps them coming
        week by week,
& nothing asks
        but "thanks."

My teeth, my eyes,
        my memory,
my legs, my way
        with words
depend on his
        first aid.

She lifts me up,
        & down me lays;
I move around
        in his embrace.

The Sea of Life

It's easier for whales
    & small fishes
to fall out of
    the wide
    wide sea,
than it is, O mighty Lord,
    for any one of us,
    thine own
    progeny,
to fall out of life
    in thee.

People

Abraham

There is but one house of God—
   one mosque,
   one church,
   one synagogue
with many varied expressions
   in the many sects
   of Judaism,
   Christianity,
   & Islam.

At least, that's my view,
   & I suspect
   Jesus,
   Moses,
   & Muhammad
   thought so, too.

Though we may prefer
   one over another,
   from day
   to day,
we can still acknowledge all
   as sisters
   & brothers,

part of a single human family,
   that springs
   from one
   common
   scriptural
     r
     o
     o
     t
     .

The Child

—In memory of Phillips Brooks*

At about age twenty-nine,
    I found I wanted
      so much more
      of life,
& expected so much more
    from life,
that there was no way
    it could be
    discovered
outside the confines
    of God,
    & angels,
& all things divine.

That's why & when
    I finally let
"the dear Christ"
    enter in.

*See "O Little Town of Bethlehem"

The Babe

We're coloring our eggs
    on Easter week,
expecting the babe
    of Bethlehem
to break out from his night
    in Plato's cave
& drench the whole world
    in transcendent light.

The Son of Man

> *. . . and they shall see the Son of man coming in
> the clouds of heaven with power and great glory.*
> Matt 24:30

Surprise, surprise!
    Awaited truth
    arrives
astride a cloud—
    & so,
we must expect
    the cold
& darkest hour
    just before
the crack of dawn,
    & behind
each little silver lining
    a suddenly
    shining
    sun.

Jesus' Blood

Jesus was bleeding
    something above
    our common sense
    of human blood—
a hemorrhaging excess
    of the dear
    Father-Mother's
    all-absorbing love.

Mary, Mary

Neither forgetting nor forgotten,
    an angelic expectancy of good
is its own bright motherhood,
    the good begetting good.

If this precious rule were
    widely understood,
& never then forsaken,
    so many would be blessed:
both us & the great Begetter,
    plus all our beloved babes,
so *consciously* begotten.

Fishers of Men

The apostles of God
    are not actually
    of the human race
    or any other form
of competition—
    "in but not *of*"
    this world
of hipsters, hucksters,
    & professional
    fishers,
at least not those
    who fish
    for riches,
    for fame,
    for food,
or even for fishes.

Gentle Plato

I hope it might please
    gentle Plato
to note some symmetry
    between
his allegory of the cave
    & the shadow
    of death
    in Psalm 23.

I think of his sun
    as a symbol
    of Love,
    pouring out light
to manacled sight
    from the realm
    of Spirit
    & eternal life.

Luther

Luther wrote what
    the Spirit said,
*Ja oder **Nein?***

Then he did
    as the Spirit bid,
*Ja oder **Nein?***

Did he suffer
    for the trouble?
*Ja oh **Ja!***

Did he know
    where it led?
Nein** oh **Nein!

Did this then give him
    a voice divine?
*Ja oder **Nein?***

Prayer

The Hug

My morning hug
    is no big deal;
we do this
    every day.

I can't express
    what I feel;
I know not
    what to say.

I just give God
    my gratitude,
& she says
    we are good.

Elevating Thought

Jesus says to enter
    our closet
& then to close
    that door.

These soul zones
    are elevators
for uplifting thought
    & prayer.

The trick's to firmly
    bar the door,
so we don't pass up
    our chance to soar.

Reconciled

When we live in Love
    & it's in us,
the world explodes
    in loveliness.

For this we pray
    & atone:
to dwell in Love
    & Love alone—

that we may grow
    to be spot clean,
an image of
    the One supreme.

Gabriel

When a terrible storm
    seems to be brewing,
ask gentle Gabriel
    to blow his horn.
No sounds are more bright
    or brilliantly stark
than this angel blasting
    into the dark.

Like Little Boy Blue,
    raising his horn,
when "sheep's in the meadow,"
    "cow's in the corn,"
or some lovely grace notes
    lifting a score,
Gabe tames the thunder
    today as of yore.

Face Time

Try a little face time
        with Love,
        divine,
in daylight or at night,
        & see
        if you
don't speedily discern
        your heart
        & soul—
if not your facial skin—
        begin to burn
        or *glow.*

The Oasis

The shore of tomorrow
    is a divine oasis
a place for all to wash—
    no sand
    no second hand
    or calendar,
an eternal hour's watch,
    a golden
    mental
    mine
replete with love,
    where
space & time
    dissolve.

The Oath

I swear to expect,
    respect,
& to try to see
    in all others
the exact image of God,
    the full image,
    & nothing
    but this image,
so help me, God.

Lance the Lesser

What I most want
    & pray
    to be:
less of Lance,
    but more
    of me,
the spitting image
    of Love,
    Divinity.

Homing

Overhead,
    a little south
    of grand Seattle,
as the weak & weary
    start to tumble
    into bed
at workday's end,
    we hear lugubrious
    radar-aided
    jumbo jets
blindly rumble up our skyway
    into ordered flight.

Then, too, from far out
    on soupy
    Puget Sound,
    low foghorns
in our jaded ears resound,
    warning
ships & crews
    left & right
of dangers shrouded
    from restricted sight.

So, before we quit electric light,
     & our tired bodies
     seek resort
in dark zones of uncharted sleep,
     we ask the one good
     merciful Mind
to keep, guard, & guide
     to their home ports
all who sojourn, all who fight,
     through this mental
     hinge of night.

So Be It

I used to say "amen,"
      meaning: "So be it,"
though seldom it was so.

Then, I decided it meant
      "That does it!"
& it more often did.

So, now I try not
      to reach "amen"
before I'm sure I *mean* it.

At-one-ment

Love's a science
    & an art,
whose rules seem easy
    at the start;
it's practice that's
    the sticky part.

Till we feel totally
    at one with Love,
we can't be certain
    our work is done.

Practice

Bonanza

When we eat manna,
    today is *mañana*,
& with this present,
    we must rest content.

Spiritual Archaeology

Spiritual archaeology
    is the prayerful,
    mindful study
of the hidden pre-history
    & post-history
    of mankind—
an entirely pre-Genesis,
    post-Apocalypse
    reality
beyond all space or time,
    which presupposes
    "peace on earth,
goodwill to man" eternally.

Delight

There's little joy
     in fear
     or night,
but when dawns
     mentally
the eternal light,
     we know
     & feel
Love's deep delight.

Daily Tithe

Should this be my daily tithe?
O Lord of life, to thee:
that I return in energy
one-tenth supplied to me?

Or should this be my daily tithe,
O source of love divine:
I save for thee in affection
one-tenth thou makest mine?

Or should this be my little tithe:
One-tenth the creativity
lavished day to day on me
I exercise to honor thee?

This & more I might remit,
if thy nature would permit
measurement in percent.
But what's a tenth of *infinity*?

The Furnace

Shadrach, Meshach,
    & Abednego
should all of us inspire:

They show that Love
    can shield us
right in the midst of fire.

Your Heart

Where your treasure lies,
    a wise man said,
there your little heart
    also flies.

Where's your temple?
    Who built it?
What treasures
    have you there?

Do you keep them
    all locked up
like stocks & bonds
    in a safety box?

How safe are they?
    How liquid?
Will they pay
    dividends,
when the body's dead?

Defense of a Prophet

Of some ancient
    & extremely
    wise prophet,
they used to comment
    to his doubtful
    students
that he was not
    so much
    absent
as *other* minded.

Come Out

You're not yet
    who you
    really are,
nor, in fact,
    am I;
that we should know.

Nonetheless, we're acting out
    our daily roles,
    full force,
    full time,
as if dress rehearsing
    for some
    grand show.

When we've finally
    outgrown
these dramatis personae,
    we'll all
    be better
at baring our souls—
    & find in our
    now-righteous play
meanings sublime.

The New Man

I am the man
    I am,
not the man
    I was:
unsure,
    unjust,
dismayed.

My future
    is for
I Am
    to say:
his/hers
    to reveal;
mine only
    to explore.

My Castle Home

My castle home is
    divinely mental
    with room for all
    my friends & foes.

There's no one that
    it cannot fit,
    nor find a place
    where one can sit.

I've been adding rooms
    as time goes by:
    space for meetings,
    places to cry.

The more I do this
    & let people know,
    the more blessed I feel,
    & content I grow.

Empowered

As children of the Lord,
    there's nothing,
      nada,
we can't in the end
    perform
    or master—
for the power
    profound
    of our
consciousness of God
    is the one
    & only
Conquistador.

Our Music Never Ends

Does the music stop
    when a concert
    or a season
grinds to its "inevitable" end?

No, it lives on, lingers,
    & is often revived—
    played out over
    & over again
from time to time
    in grateful hearts.

Quite similarly, the melodies
    of those
    with whom
we've worked & played,
    & somehow
    harmonized,
are indelibly recorded
    in our memories
& constantly reprised,
    shared with others;

so that the symphonies
    of all
our mingled lives
    reside
    forever
& forever resound
    in listening hearts
    & open minds.

Made in the USA
Las Vegas, NV
05 December 2022

61219602R00042